For Mabel George

First published in Great Britain in 2004 by
Frances Lincoln Children's Books, 4 Torriano Mews
Torriano Avenue, London NW5 2RZ
www.franceslincoln.com
Distributed in the USA by Publishers Group West

British Library Cataloguing in Publication Data
available on request

ISBN 1-84507-007-0

Printed in Singapore
1 3 5 7 9 8 6 4 2

PARADISE

Fiona French

FRANCES LINCOLN CHILDREN'S BOOKS

In the beginning God created the heaven and the earth. And the earth was without form; and darkness was upon the face of the deep.

And the spirit of God moved upon the face of the waters. And God said, "Let there be light," and there was light. And God called the light Day, and the darkness he called Night.

And God said, "Let there be a firmament in the midst of the waters." And God called the firmament Heaven.

And God said, "Let the waters under the heaven be gathered together, and let the dry land appear." God called the dry land Earth, and the waters he called Seas; and God saw that it was good.

And God said, "Let the earth bring forth grass, the herb yielding seed, and the fruit tree yielding fruit."

And God made two great lights:
    the greater light to rule the day,
and the lesser light to rule the night;
he also made the stars.

And God created great whales,
and every living creature that moveth,
and every winged fowl. And God blessed them,
saying, "Be fruitful and multiply."

And the Lord God created man in his own image;
God formed man of the dust of the ground
and breathed into his nostrils the breath of life;
male and female created he them.

And on the seventh day
God rested from all his work.

And the Lord God planted a garden eastward of Eden; and there he put the man whom he had formed, saying, "Of every tree of the garden thou mayest freely eat: but of the tree of the knowledge of good and evil, thou shalt not eat, for thou shalt surely die."

Now the serpent was more subtle than
any beast of the field which the Lord God
had made, and he said unto the woman,
"Ye shall not surely die: ye shall be as gods,
knowing good and evil."

And when the woman saw that the tree was good for food, she took of the fruit and did eat, and gave also to her husband.

And the eyes of both of them were opened, and they knew that they were naked, and they hid themselves amongst the trees of the garden.

And the Lord God called unto Adam,
"Where art thou? Who told thee thou
wast naked? Hast thou eaten of the tree?"
And the woman said, "The serpent beguiled me,
and I did eat."

And the Lord God said unto the serpent,
"Thou art cursed. Upon thy belly shalt
thou go, and dust shalt thou eat
all the days of thy life."

Unto Adam and his wife did the Lord God make coats of skins, and clothed them.

And the Lord God said, "Behold, lest the man take also of the tree of life, and live for ever," therefore he sent them forth from the garden of Eden.

And he placed at the east of the garden cherubims, and a flaming sword to keep the way of the tree of life.